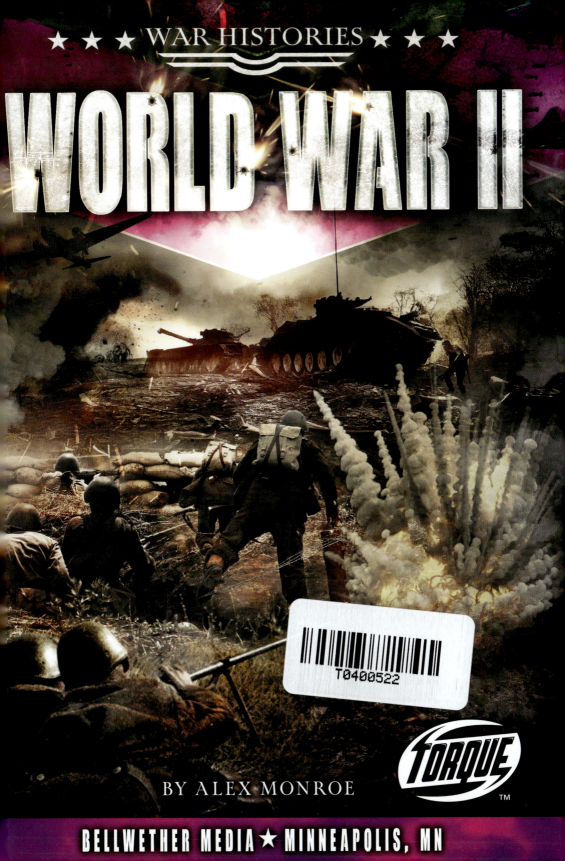

Torque brims with excitement perfect for thrill-seekers of all kinds. Discover daring survival skills, explore uncharted worlds, and marvel at mighty engines and extreme sports. In *Torque* books, anything can happen. Are you ready?

This edition first published in 2024 by Bellwether Media, Inc.

No part of this publication may be reproduced in whole or in part without written permission of the publisher. For information regarding permission, write to Bellwether Media, Inc., Attention: Permissions Department, 6012 Blue Circle Drive, Minnetonka, MN 55343.

Library of Congress Cataloging-in-Publication Data

Names: Monroe, Alex (Writer of children's books), author.
Title: World War II / by Alex Monroe.
Other titles: World War Two
Description: Minneapolis, MN : Bellwether Media, Inc., 2024. | Series: Torque : War histories | Includes bibliographical references and index. | Audience: Ages 7-12 | Audience: Grades 4-6 | Summary: "Engaging images accompany information about World War II. The combination of high-interest subject matter and light text is intended for students in grades 3 through 7"– Provided by publisher.
Identifiers: LCCN 2023007739 (print) | LCCN 2023007740 (ebook) | ISBN 9798886874556 (library binding) | ISBN 9798886875478 (paperback) | ISBN 9798886876437 (ebook)
Subjects: LCSH: World War, 1939-1945–Juvenile literature.
Classification: LCC D743.7 .M65 2024 (print) | LCC D743.7 (ebook) | DDC 940.53–dc23/eng/20230302
LC record available at https://lccn.loc.gov/2023007739
LC ebook record available at https://lccn.loc.gov/2023007740

Text copyright © 2024 by Bellwether Media, Inc. TORQUE and associated logos are trademarks and/or registered trademarks of Bellwether Media, Inc.

Editor: Elizabeth Neuenfeldt   Designer: Josh Brink

Printed in the United States of America, North Mankato, MN.

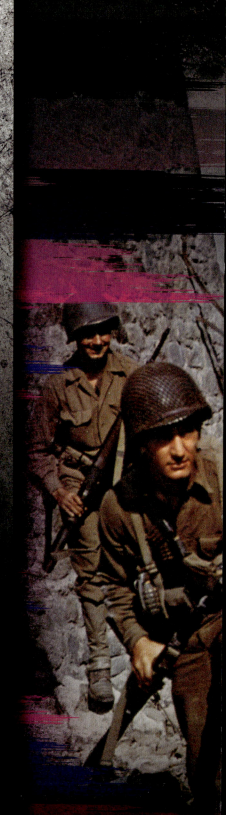

TABLE OF CONTENTS

WHAT WAS WORLD WAR II?	4
AXIS INVASION	6
THE WORLD AT WAR	10
TURNING THE TIDE	14
THE AFTERMATH	18
GLOSSARY	22
TO LEARN MORE	23
INDEX	24

WHAT WAS WORLD WAR II?

World War II lasted from 1939 to 1945. It was fought between two big **alliances**. They were the **Axis powers** and the **Allied powers**.

Fighting mostly took place in Europe and the Pacific Ocean. Almost every country in the world was involved. It was the largest and deadliest war in history.

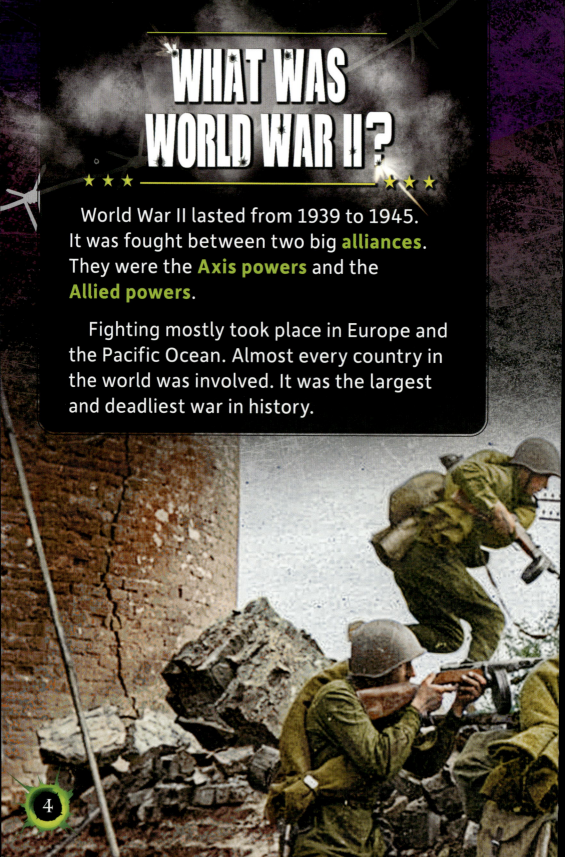

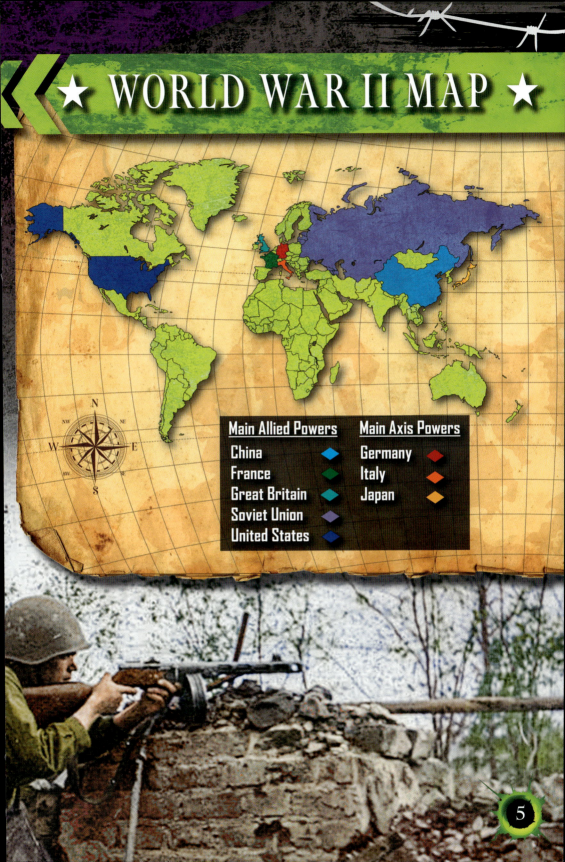

AXIS INVASION

World War I ended in 1918. Germany lost. The country lost land. It ran out of money. Germans struggled to live.

GERMAN SOUP KITCHEN

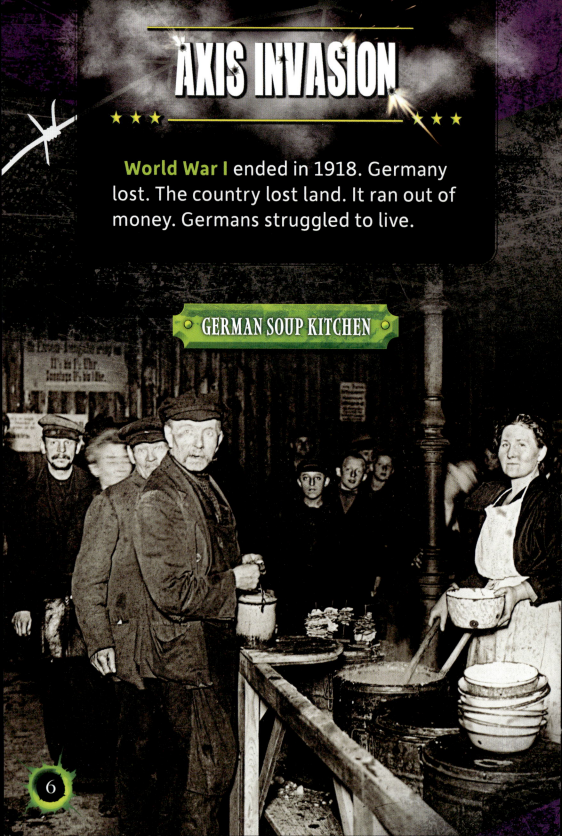

In 1933, Adolf Hitler came to power in Germany. He blamed certain people for Germany's problems. He ordered the **Nazis** to remove **Jewish** people, **Roma** people, and many others. Later, he ordered them killed. These horrific actions during the war became known as the **Holocaust**.

AXIS LEADER

NAME
Adolf Hitler

NATIONALITY
Austrian, German

POSITION
Chancellor of Germany (1933 to 1945); Führer of Germany (1934 to 1945)

IMPORTANT ACTIONS
- 1933: Became Chancellor of Germany
- 1939: Invaded Poland
- 1940: Took control of most of Western Europe

Hitler wanted to control Europe. Nazis began to **invade** nearby lands. Leaders in Italy and Japan also wanted more land. They took over nearby countries, too. In time, Germany, Italy, and Japan formed the Axis powers.

On September 1, 1939, Germany invaded Poland. Both sides called on other countries for help. World War II had begun.

ALLIED LEADER

NAME
Franklin Delano Roosevelt

NATIONALITY
American

POSITION
U.S. President (1933 to 1945)

IMPORTANT ACTIONS
- 1941 to 1945: Helped form the United Nations
- 1941: Led the U.S. to war against Japan
- 1943 to 1944: Helped plan D-Day

THE WORLD AT WAR

Germany and Italy won many battles early in the war. Axis forces made large, fast attacks. Allied forces struggled to defend themselves. By June 1940, Nazi Germany controlled most of Western Europe.

LONDON AFTER A GERMAN AIR RAID

WINSTON CHURCHILL

Germany tried to take over Great Britain with **air raids**. Many **civilians** died. Cities were destroyed. But Great Britain stood strong. Its leader, Winston Churchill, gave many people hope.

Meanwhile, Japan invaded much of Southeast Asia. Great Britain, France, and the Netherlands were busy fighting in Europe. They lost lands they controlled in Southeast Asia to Japan.

Then, on December 7, 1941, Japan attacked the U.S. forces in Pearl Harbor, Hawaii. The next day, the U.S. decided to declare war on Japan. They would fight many battles in the Pacific.

ATTACK ON PEARL HARBOR

JAPANESE AMERICANS

During the war, U.S. leaders feared Japanese Americans would help Japan. There was no proof. But the U.S. forced Japanese Americans into camps. From 1942 to 1946, around 120,000 people were held in these camps.

★ THE WAR AT HOME ★

Civilians on both sides were in danger of air raids. Sirens warned people enemy aircraft were near. People hid in shelters to stay safe.

Food and supplies went to soldiers. Families struggled to get food. Most soldiers were men. Women took over jobs usually held by men. Many women made weapons in factories.

PRACTICING FOR AIR RAIDS IN LONDON

TURNING THE TIDE

★★★ ─────────── ★★★

In June 1942, Japan tried to attack U.S. forces on the island of Midway. But the U.S. learned what was going to happen. The U.S. made its own surprise attack.

After days of fighting, Japanese forces lost. It was the first important win for the Allies in the Pacific. They continued to win more battles.

WORLD WAR II TIMELINE

September 1, 1939
Germany invades Poland

December 7, 1941
Japan attacks Pearl Harbor

June 4, 1942
The Battle of Midway begins

NAVAJO CODE TALKERS

During the war, U.S. Marines from the Navajo Nation made a code. It was based on the Navajo language. It helped the Allies talk over radios without enemies knowing what they said. The code was never broken!

June 6, 1944 — D-Day begins

May 7, 1945 — Germany surrenders, ending the war in Europe

September 2, 1945 — Japan surrenders

BATTLE OF STALINGRAD

In August 1942, the Battle of Stalingrad began. It was the deadliest battle of the war. But the Allies won in 1943. Later that year, Italy **surrendered**.

On June 6, 1944, over 160,000 Allied soldiers attacked Axis forces in Normandy, France. It was called D-Day. The battle helped free Europe from Nazi Germany.

THE AFTERMATH

By 1945, Axis forces were weak. On May 7, Germany surrendered. The war in Europe was over.

Fighting continued in Asia. On August 6, the U.S. dropped an **atomic bomb** on Hiroshima, Japan. Three days later, the U.S. dropped another bomb on Nagasaki, Japan. Thousands of civilians died. Japan surrendered on September 2, 1945.

"LITTLE BOY" ATOMIC BOMB

Weight:
around 9,700 pounds (4,400 kilograms)

Power:
equal to around 15,000 tons (13,608 metric tons) of TNT

Length:
120 inches (305 centimeters)

Destruction to Hiroshima:
around 7 out of every 10 buildings destroyed

HIROSHIMA AFTER THE ATOMIC BOMB

The war destroyed many cities. Millions of people died. Six million Jewish people and millions of others were killed in the Holocaust alone. **Memorials** and museums were made worldwide to honor Holocaust victims and survivors. They make sure people's stories are remembered.

Countries began working together to help prevent wars. In 1945, the **United Nations** formed. It keeps peace around the world.

HOLOCAUST MEMORIAL

★ BY THE NUMBERS ★

250,000 people = 👤

ESTIMATED NUMBER OF SOLDIERS KILLED IN BATTLE
- 15 million

ESTIMATED NUMBER OF SOLDIERS INJURED
- 25 million

ESTIMATED NUMBER OF CIVILIANS KILLED
- 45 million

NUMBER OF U.S. MILITARY PERSONNEL DEPLOYED
- 16 million

COST OF WWII TO THE U.S.
- nearly $5 trillion dollars (in 2020 dollars)

NUMBER OF PEOPLE WHO LOST THEIR HOMES IN EUROPE
- 60 million

GLOSSARY

air raids—attacks from above made by armed airplanes

alliances—friendships between countries; allies usually support each other in times of war.

Allied powers—an alliance between Great Britain, the Soviet Union, China, France, the United States, and other countries during World War II

atomic bomb—a deadly bomb powered by the energy released when certain atoms are split

Axis powers—an alliance between Nazi Germany, Italy, Japan, and other countries during World War II

civilians—people who do not belong to a nation's armed forces

Holocaust—the killing of millions of Jewish people and other people groups by the Nazis in World War II

invade—to enter a land to control it

Jewish—related to people who came from the ancient Hebrew people; Jewish can also refer to people who practice the religion of Judaism.

memorials—places that serve as reminders of events or people

Nazis—members of a German political party that controlled Germany from 1933 to 1945

Roma—an ethnic group of traditionally nomadic people who originated in India and now live all over the world

surrendered—gave up and decided to lose

United Nations—a political group formed in 1945 that works around the world to maintain peace

World War I—a war from 1914 to 1918 that involved many countries

TO LEARN MORE

AT THE LIBRARY

Hopkinson, Deborah. *D-Day: The World War II Invasion that Changed History.* New York, N.Y.: Scholastic Focus, 2018.

Katz, Susan B. *The History of Pearl Harbor: A World War II Book for New Readers.* Emeryville, Calif.: Rockridge Press, 2021.

Shackleton, Kath, ed. *Survivors of the Holocaust.* Naperville, Ill.: Sourcebooks Explore, 2019.

ON THE WEB

Factsurfer.com gives you a safe, fun way to find more information.

1. Go to www.factsurfer.com

2. Enter "World War II" into the search box and click 🔍.

3. Select your book cover to see a list of related content.

INDEX

air raids, 11, 13
Allied powers, 4, 5, 9, 10, 14, 15, 16
atomic bomb, 18, 19
Axis powers, 4, 5, 8, 10, 16, 18
Battle of Midway, 14
Battle of Stalingrad, 16
by the numbers, 21
Churchill, Winston, 11
civilians, 11, 13, 18
D-Day, 16, 17
deaths, 11, 18, 20
Europe, 4, 8, 10, 12, 16, 18
France, 12, 16
Germany, 6, 7, 8, 10, 11, 16, 18
Great Britain, 11, 12
Hiroshima, Japan, 18, 19
Hitler, Adolf, 7, 8
Holocaust, 7, 20
Italy, 8, 10, 16
Japan, 8, 12, 13, 14, 18
Japanese Americans, 13
Jewish people, 7, 20
leaders, 8, 9
map, 5, 17
Nagasaki, Japan, 18
Navajo Code Talkers, 15
Nazis, 7, 8, 10, 16
Netherlands, 12
Normandy, France, 16
Pacific Ocean, 4, 12, 14
Pearl Harbor, 12
Poland, 8
Roma people, 7
Roosevelt, Franklin Delano, 9
Southeast Asia, 12, 18
timeline, 14–15
United Nations, 20
United States, 12, 13, 14, 15, 18
war at home, 13
World War I, 6

The images in this book are reproduced through the courtesy of: Cassowary Colorizations/ Wikimedia Commons, front cover (bottom left soldiers), pp. 4-5; NatUlrich, front cover (left middle soldier ditch); Alexyz3d, front cover (right explosion); Sergey Kamshylin, front cover (middle right soldiers); Design Projects, front cover (tanks); Everett Collection, front cover (planes and bombing); United Kingdom Government/ Wikimedia Commons, front cover (left plane); MPVHistory/ Alamy, pp. 2-3, 22-24; FPG/ Staff/ Getty Images, pp. 6-7; World History Archive/ Alamy, pp. 7, 11, 18-19; Pictorial Press/ Alamy, pp. 8, 9; World of Triss/ Alamy, p. 10; Chronicle/ Alamy, p. 11 (Churchill); Science History Images/ Alamy, pp. 12-13; CBW/ Alamy, p. 13; National Archives Catalog, pp. 14 (1941), 14-15; carlo maggio/ Alamy, p. 14 (1939); MickStephenson/ Wikimedia Commons, p. 15 (1944); akg-images/ Alamy, p. 16; Robert F. Sargent/ Wikimedia Commons, p. 17; National Museum of the United States Air Force/ Wikimedia Commons, p. 19; anandoart, pp. 20-21; Kamila Koziol, back cover.